St Andrews in the 50s, 60s and 70s

Helen Cook

Donkeys on the West Sands in the summer of 1959.

George Cowie took this fine character study of a St Andrews soutar in May 1951. Thomas Clegg, craftsman shoemaker and repairer, lived and worked at 86 North Street. He repaired shoes for our family.

ACKNOWLEDGEMENTS

The author wishes to thank the University of St Andrews' department of special collections and rare books and its staff for research facilities, particularly Dr Norman Reid, Head of Special Collections, Cilla Jackson and Pam Cranston, for their cooperation and help in sourcing the photographs. Thanks also to the late Douglas Hamilton, Dennis Martin, Grant Milne, the British Golf Museum, St Andrews Museum and W.L. Watson & Sons.

FURTHER READING

With the exception of *Old St Andrews*, none of the following titles are available from Stenlake Publishing.

Ronald G. Cant et al, *Three Decades of Historical Notes*, compiled by Mary M. Innes and Joan Whelan, St Andrews Preservation Trust 1991
Ronald G. Cant, *The University of St Andrews, A Short History*, 3rd edition, 1992
Helen Cook, *Old St Andrews*, 2001
St Andrews Citizen

Articles by the author published in *The Scots* magazine and other periodicals and newspapers have played their part in the writing of this book, along with personal recollections.

Text © Helen Cook, 2008
Images © University of St Andrews 2008
First published in the United Kingdom, 2008,
by Stenlake Publishing Ltd.
www.stenlake.co.uk
ISBN 9781840334234

INTRODUCTION

Until the Reformation the Royal Burgh of St Andrews was the ecclesiastical capital of Scotland. Today St Andrews' medieval street plan is still intact in the heart of the town, and is complemented by the ruined cathedral, the great Church of St Andrew (1160) and its episcopal palace, the now ruined St Andrews Castle. The town is also home to Scotland's oldest university, founded in 1410–14.

Modern St Andrews is a historic tapestry of old and new and reflects the cultural evolution of Scotland over many centuries. With its tranquil setting of sea, sands and green links, it is a busy cosmopolitan town with a population of 15,000, plus about 7,000 students.

The 1950s, 60s and 70s were decades of change in St Andrews, characterised by significant population growth and much building work. In 1951 the population stood at 9,457, rising to 11,480 in 1971 (excluding students). During the 60s and 70s the university embarked on a substantial building programme, and student numbers rose from 2,000 in 1967–8 to 3,000 in 1972–3.

Against a backdrop of increasing car ownership and the opening of the Forth Road Bridge (1964) and the Tay Road Bridge (1966), the St Andrews / Guardbridge / Leuchars Junction railway line closed on 6 January 1969. With this gone, St Andrews was the only town of any size in Fife without a railway link – at a time when it was growing in size.

The university's expansion included the development of the North Haugh as a science precinct. By 1972 this former greenfield site had become home to the physical sciences building, the mathematical institute, the chemistry / geography building and the computational science building. In Union Street the Buchanan Building (for modern languages) was completed in 1964, its Market Street frontage occupying the site of the a famous old tenement known as the 'Double Decker'. A new university library was completed in North Street in 1976. Additional student housing was also built during this period, including Andrew Melville Hall.

During the period covered by this book, four new local authority schools were built: Langlands Primary (1957), Canongate Primary (1971), Lawhead Primary (1974) and Kilrymont, the Madras junior school (1967). The latter created a split-site school with senior pupils in the original 1832 building (with later additions) in South Street. None of the new schools were in the old part of St Andrews, which was declared a conservation area in 1971.

In 1954 an acute shortage of private houses for rent in St Andrews, combined with long waiting lists for council houses, prompted the town council to commission around 100 new homes. From the 1960s private housing on greenfield sites was developed at the Canongate, Claybraes, Hallowhill, Irvine Crescent and other parts of the town.

In tandem with the building of new houses, many period properties in the old part of the town were renovated by the St Andrews Preservation Trust (local pioneers in this field), private individuals and the town council. Between 1970 and 1973 the council carried out a notable renovation of two historic South Street properties, 'The Great Eastern' (bearing the coat of arms of Prior Hepburn), and South Court (bearing the coat of arms of the Martine family). The renovated buildings provided flats for older people.

One of the most important events of this period was the passing of the Local Government (Scotland) Act of 1973, as a result of which North-East Fife District Council was set up. This led to the demise of St Andrews Town Council in 1975. The town's provost at the time was Dr John B. Gilchrist. A retired Madras College teacher, he was the last in a long line of St Andrews provosts dating back to Mainard the Fleming in the twelfth century.

During the period covered here, St Andrews had a wide range of local shops and businesses including grocers, butchers, bakers, fishmongers, fruiterers and chemists. Many familiar names are recalled on the following pages. Never an industrial town, the St Andrews economy in the 1950s, 60s and 70s was based – as it is today – on its university, golf and the tourist and conference industry.

These images from the relatively recent past show a town that has changed significantly but is still readily recognisable. It is hoped that they will stimulate memories for local people, and provide a new perspective on the town for those new to the area.

About the photographs

The images in this book were all taken by George Cowie and come from the Cowie Collection, part of the photographic archive of the University of St Andrews.

George Middlemass Cowie (1902–82, the son of an East Lothian joiner) and his wife Beatrice Govan, were both skilled professional photographers who traded in St Andrews for over half a century from 1929. George Cowie was primarily a press photographer, his apprenticeship coinciding with the earliest period of photojournalism. He documented life in St Andrews, north-east Fife and the rest of the 'Kingdom' in all its variety.

Golf at St Andrews and elsewhere played an important part in George Cowie's professional life, and he loved to photograph the famous faces who came to play in the town. Additionally, he and his photographer son Andrew (d.1980) took the official photographs of the Byre Theatre's productions for approaching fifty years. The theatre was founded by George's friend and journalist colleague, A.B. Paterson. George Cowie was also supportive of the St Andrews Preservation Trust, and made a series of prints for them, creating a visual record of changes within the old town in recent times. He continued to work as a press photographer until shortly before his death.

St Andrews stonemason Andrew Watson carving a gargoyle out of Blaxter sandstone during repair work to Holy Trinity Church in January 1969. Andrew was employed by W.L. Watson & Sons, a local firm of stonemasons who are known for their historic buildings restoration work. Holy Trinity Church – also known as the 'Town Kirk' – was founded in South Street in 1410–12. It replaced an earlier parish church which stood near the east gable of the cathedral and dated to at least 1163. A burial ground originally occupied land to the north and south of today's Holy Trinity Church, and for at least two hundred years the churchyard wall extended along what is now the middle of South Street. During the renovation of St Andrews public library in Church Square (completed in 2004), archaeological evidence of this old burial ground was found.

Winter spells of continuous hard frost once saw the ground adjoining the greens of the St Andrews Bowling Club flooded for skating. Here on a January day in 1958 pupils from St Leonard's School are enjoying the frosty weather. Founded in 1877 as a private school for girls, today St Leonard's is an independent co-educational school. Before the development of nearby Southfield for housing in 1879, skating also took place on the now disappeared Southfield Pond. Although outdoor skating on temporary rinks has become a popular and fashionable form of winter exercise, St Andrews no longer has a site for this sport. Only a memory too is the sledging which once took place at the North Haugh adjoining Jacob's Ladder. This ceased when St Andrews University began to develop the area as a science precinct in the mid-1960s. In the background on the left is the bowling club's pavilion in Kinnessburn Road. The bowling green was badly damaged in the 1942 bombing of Nelson Street.

A 1959 photograph showing Mrs Allen operating machinery at the St Andrews Weaving Co., 125 Market Street. The workshop was located in a small complex of former bakery buildings behind the erstwhile shop and tea-room of Elder the bakers. Elder's bakehouse was accessed by a pend at the side of the shop, and freshly baked rolls could be bought there before the shop opened in the morning. Since the photograph was taken this part of Market Street has seen both redevelopment and changes to the street frontage.

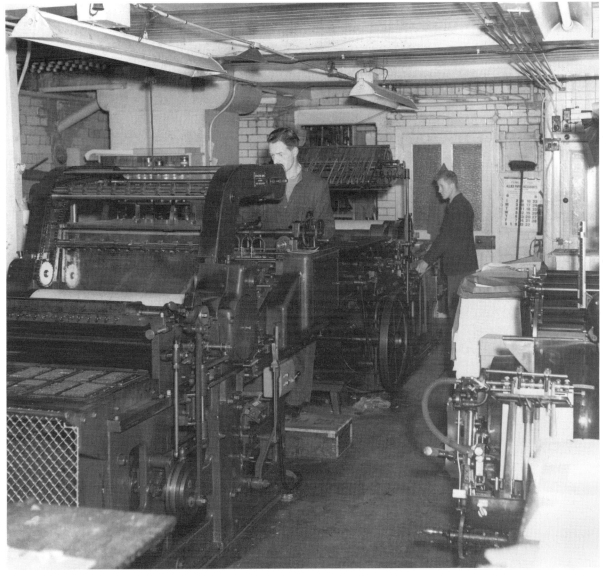

Printing presses belonging to W.C. Henderson, university printers and stationers, photographed in February 1958. The firm was founded in 1855 by Mr W.C. Henderson and became a limited company in 1927. In 1865 it was located at 5 Church Street and described itself as a 'bookseller with circulating library'. Henderson's printworks were at 80 Market Street, where the company also had a sports shop. This site had a long association with printing and publishing. In a much earlier building at 80 Market Street, Joseph Cook & Son (established in the eighteenth century) were in business as booksellers, stationers, bookbinders, printers and publishers. Cook's published an early local paper called the *St Andrews Citizen & East Coast Advertiser*. This came out on a Saturday, price one penny. Today the upper stories of Henderson's former building at 80 Market Street are flats, while the old sports shop is still a retail unit. Henderson's also had a large shop at 19 Church Street which sold books and stationery and was often referred to as the university bookshop. Tickets for the Byre Theatre could also be bought or booked at Henderson's.

This North Street building was called College Gate for obvious reasons. It was used as the administrative offices of St Andrews University from 1944 until 1949, when it was demolished to make way for a larger building. Plans to enlarge the old building had to be abandoned when the structure was found to be unsound. The new building, also called College Gate, entered service as university office accommodation in 1953.

A stonemason photographed by George Cowie working on the site of the new College Gate in March 1950. The town's Episcopal Chapel – sometimes called the English Chapel – stood in this area from 1824–70. Dedicated to St Andrew, it was superseded in 1869 by the much larger St Andrew's Episcopal Church in Queen's Terrace. The redundant North Street building was then sold to the Free Church in Buckhaven. Every stone was numbered and the church was dismantled and shipped from St Andrews harbour to Buckhaven in the thirty-ton steamer *Hemija* of Anstruther. St Andrews tradesmen did the plastering and plumbing in the re-erected church. It still stands today and is now used as a theatre.

Having fun for a good cause! Until 1985, St Andrews University students held colourful annual fundraising campaigns with a procession featuring a Charities Queen. Funds were raised for local and national good causes. This photograph of the 1949 campaign shows students in North Street on a 1901 Merryweather fire engine, gifted to St Andrews by Major Donald Lindsay Carnegie (d.1911). In the left background, at No. 87, are the business premises of J.K. Wilson, a golfing friend of Bing Crosby. These were later occupied by builder Angus M. MacDougall. Both No. 87 and the neighbouring hall of the Eastern Star were demolished to provide ground for the Crawford Centre and an entrance to the new university library, opened in 1976.

The 1960 Charities Queen poses with two students about to embark on a fundraising scooter race from St Salvator's College. Note the collecting can, a vital feature of such events!

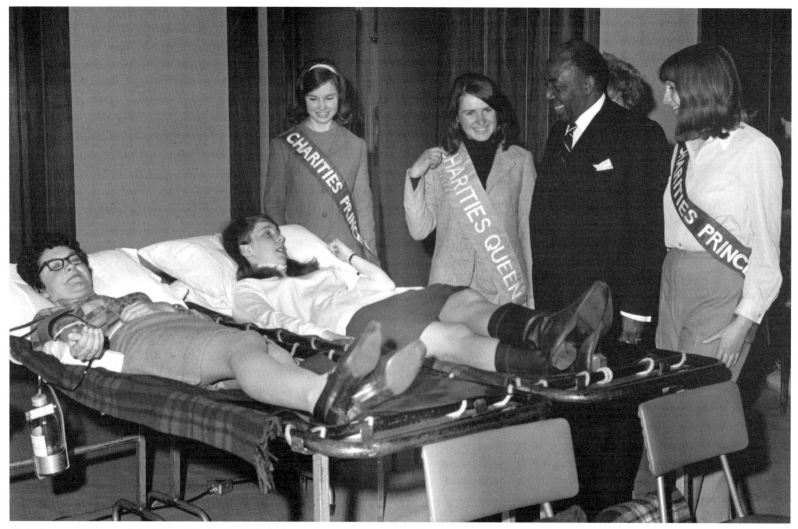

St Andrews students giving blood in April 1968 during a charities campaign. Showing support is the famous cricketer, politician and barrister, Baron Learie Constantine (1901–71), who was elected Rector of St Andrews University in 1967. Born in Trinidad, he served on the Race Relations Board and became a governor of the BBC.

Members of St Andrews Fire Brigade washing away oil following a tanker leak in North Street in September 1975. They are standing in part of the town's old fishing quarter, known as the Ladyhead or Leddyheid. This was home to a lively working community until the early years of the twentieth century. The north side of the street, from a little west of today's Younger Hall to the war memorial at the cathedral, was characterised by stone houses in a variety of vernacular styles. Along with a few similar buildings on the south side of the street, these were among the oldest houses in St Andrews and featured an assortment of thatched, red pantiled and slated roofs. Many had outside stairs and crow-stepped gables. A reminder of the fishing quarter days survives in the form of a large barometer called 'Vice-admiral Fitzroy's storm tubes' which can be seen on the wall of the Ladyhead Bookshop. This gave fishermen advance warning of bad weather. From 1827–65, the Burgher Kirk (now the site of a block of flats) occupied a chapel at 52 North Street before relocating to Hope Park Church. By that time the Burgher Kirk had become part of the United Presbyterian Kirk. On the left is the university's Gannochy Hall, and beyond the rectory of All Saints Episcopal Church. Younger Hall (obscured by the trees), Gannochy Hall and the rectory all occupy the former site of fisher houses.

This striking photograph was taken in October 1979 during the retiling of Boots the chemist, then on the west corner of the South Street / Logies Lane junction. The traditional pantiles had to be ordered from a firm in Humberside. Boots is now in Market Street and stands on the site of the Mercat Wynd shopping centre. This 1970s building formed part of the redevelopment of an area once occupied by the livery stables and garage business of William Johnston Ltd. Their premises stretched from Market Street to North Street, and included the site of today's Johnston Court. There had been a chemist's at the same location in South Street since 1822, and the crow-stepped premises of Smith & Govan, 'chemist and druggist', feature in one of the oldest photographs of St Andrews, taken in 1843. That building was demolished the same year, but following redevelopment part of it remained home to Smith & Govan until Boots took the business over. Many years ago, Logies Lane was nicknamed Coffin Lane, not because it bordered the old Holy Trinity burial ground (see page 4), but because an undertaker by the name of Berwick owned properties there.

St Andrews Town Council built a number of prefabricated houses to relieve the housing shortage following the Second World War. This photograph was taken from the junction of Priestden Place and Warrack Street in October 1956. After the war, permanent municipal housing once again began to be built. Churchill Crescent was built in 1948 and named after the great war leader and prime minister. Warrack Street took its name from Frances Jane Warrack MBE (1865–1950). Awarded an MBE for her voluntary services during the First World War, she was elected to St Andrews Town Council in 1919, and was its first woman councillor.

A 1961 photograph showing the conversion of 36 North Street into private housing. This was the former St Andrews East Poorhouse, established under the poor law legislation of 1844. The photograph shows the back of the building – known latterly as the Home of Rest – during its reconstruction. It was sited in the North Street fishing quarter of the Ladyhead (Leddyheid), and its crow-stepped gables were echoed in some of the neighbouring fisher homes. Well within living memory the Home of Rest cared for both men and women, and is remembered as a simple, clean place with floors and stairs of scrubbed wood. Some of its inmates went out and about in the community, and those who were able helped with the home's domestic chores. In 1942, when the St Andrews Women Citizens' Association (1919–1994) gave the home's occupants Christmas dinner and presents, the oldest resident was 85 and the youngest a year old.

A Royal Artillery display on the Links at St Andrews in August 1977. The Old Course Hotel is in the background. The picture is thought to show a 105mm light gun, a type first delivered to the British Army in 1975 and capable of being carried around a battlefield underslung on a Puma or Chinook helicopter. It was to prove its worth in the Falklands, where such guns sometimes fired 400 rounds per day.

This cannon belongs to the Royal and Ancient Golf Club. When the new captain of the club plays himself into office in September, the occasion is marked by the firing of the cannon at the precise moment the ball is struck. Crowds gather to watch this annual ceremony, after which the caddie who retrieves the captain's ball is presented with a gold sovereign. The cannon came from the wreck of the 1,200 ton Dundee sailing ship the *Sutlej*, which foundered with a heavy cargo in St Andrews Bay on 1 April 1858. Bound for Sydney, the *Sutlej* was a Crimean War supply ship named to commemorate the victories of the Sikh War of 1846. She left Dundee escorted by two tugs, armed for her long voyage and carrying a crew of 35 plus passengers. All went well until the *Sutlej* struck a sandbank after the pilot confused two buoys at the mouth of the River Tay. She rapidly began to take in water, and in an ebbing tide and a strong north-westerly wind was abandoned, believed to be about to sink. But instead of sinking she sailed – unmanned – across St Andrews Bay before running aground a few miles away near Kingsbarns. The cannon carries a plaque which indicates its origin and further reads 'acquired by the Club in 1859, through the offices of St Andrews Provost Sir Hugh Lyon Playfair, Captain of the Club in 1856'.

John Campbell, head green-keeper at St Andrews Links, photographed with his staff in 1970. The low, white building in the distance was the former Bay Tea Room. In the 1930s Mrs McBride provided tea, scones, ice cream and lemonade from there during the holiday season. On sunny summer days her customers could enjoy both their refreshment and the view from the roof of the cafe, accessed by an outside stair. Following alterations, the former cafe and adjoining public toilets became the first headquarters of the St Andrews Links Trust, incorporating changing rooms for golfers. The site of the building has since been absorbed into the British Golf Museum, which opened in 1990.

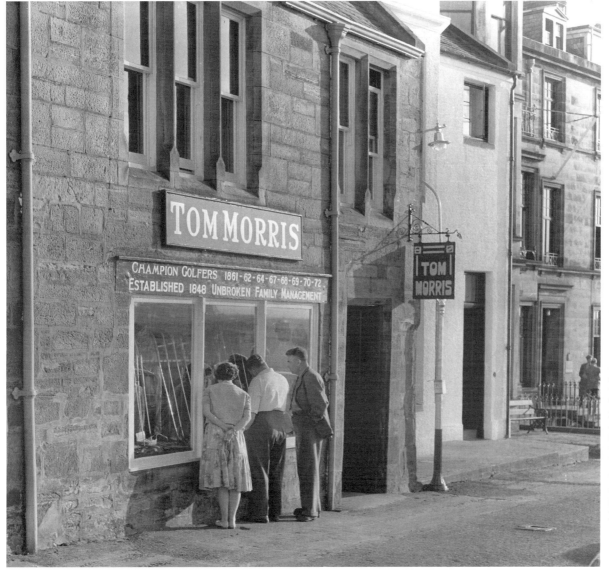

A 1959 photograph of Tom Morris's famous St Andrews golf shop, located in The Links close by the 18th green of the Old Course. Tom Morris (1821–1908) was a native of St Andrews who returned to the town from Prestwick in 1865 when the Royal and Ancient Golf Club appointed him as its green–keeper, paying him £50 a year. In addition to being four–times winner of the Open, Tom was a skilled green–keeper and course designer. He established his club and ball making business in The Links in 1866 on a site where George Daniel Brown – who played in the first Open Championship at Prestwick in 1860 – had previously had a similar business. A Tom Morris advertisement of the 1860s reads 'Thomas Morris has always on hand a complete assortment of every kind of clubs and balls used in the game. Repairs neatly and punctually executed'. Latterly Tom Morris was known as 'Old Tom' to distinguish him from his accomplished golf professional son, 'Young Tom' Morris. The shop is still open for business, and it still has a Morris connection to this day.

Eric Dalton of South Africa playing at St Andrews in June 1954. In the background are the once-famous black sheds of the old St Andrews goods station. A familiar landmark for golfers playing the Old Course, they were demolished in 1967. Today the Old Course Hotel occupies the site of the goods station. It originated as the British Transport Hotel in 1966, and has since been much enlarged, altered and updated. At one time goods stored in the black sheds included imported wood for St Andrews golf club makers.

Laurie Auchterlonie photographed in his workshop in Pilmuir Links by George Cowie in June 1966. Laurie was the only son of Willie Auchterlonie, the St Andrews clubmaker and golfer. Winner of the Open Championship at Prestwick in 1893, Willie was honorary professional to the Royal and Ancient Golf Club from 1935 until his death in 1963. Laurie was born in 1904 and attended the former Burgh School in Abbey Street, which he left at fourteen to take up a club-making apprenticeship in the family firm of D.&W. Auchterlonie. In addition to being a fine golfer, Laurie was an authority on the craft of making and restoring golf clubs, which he did with great expertise using traditional methods and materials. In 1965 he was commissioned by the Foxburg Golf Club of Pennsylvania to lay out a new golf course for them in partnership with Robert Tyre Jones – Bobby Jones. He also selected old golf clubs for the Foxburg golf museum, and went on to assist in the setting up of various golf museums and golfing halls of fame in America. He was curator of the US Golf Hall of Fame at Pinehurst. In St Andrews he helped the R&A to set up their museum, establishing his own golf museum in Pilmuir Links. Laurie Auchterlonie succeeded his father as honorary professional to the R&A, fulfilling the role until his death in 1987.

This May 1960 photograph of the St Andrews to Leuchars Junction branch line shows the 15th fairway and 16th tee of the Old Course to the left. The line opened in July 1852 and closed on 6 January 1969, even though the town council opposed its closure at every turn and there was significant resistance among residents. The council investigated the possibility of providing a subsidy to keep the line open, but at a minimum of £20,000 per year this was deemed too costly. Latterly twin diesel multiple unit trains operated the line, which was well used until the Tay Road Bridge opened in 1966.

St Andrews station photographed in July 1952 – the centenary of the formal opening of the line from Leuchars. The station was noted for its colourful floral displays. Pedestrian access was via Doubledykes Road, while the main entrance, from Station Road, featured a covered walkway with stairs down to the platform. Between 1852 and 1887 the town's passenger station was situated near the 17th hole of the Old Course and was called the Links station. The station in the photograph was built as part of the Anstruther & St Andrews Railway in 1880–87. After it opened the original station became a goods station with offices, a coal depot and engine sheds. The area seen here is now used for car parking, while the goods station has been replaced by the Old Course Hotel and the nearby Jigger Inn occupies the former stationmaster's house.

The former Star Hotel on
Market Street (demolished in
1982) opened in the nineteenth
century and provided modern
amenities for Victorian visitors
to St Andrews, including
stabling and a yard for coaches.
While the hotel's pillared
doorway has been retained, the
ground floor is now occupied
by modern shops, some with
frontages in Logies Lane. Like
the Star Hotel, Hogg's shoe
shop (left, on the former site of
the Commercial Inn) has also
closed, but the sweet shop on
the right, at the top of Logies
Lane (then owned by Mr and
Mrs Burns and previously by
Mr and Mrs Boyd) is still open
under different ownership. The
parking spaces in the
foreground mark the site of the
old townhouse/tolbooth, which
was demolished in 1862 on
completion of the new town hall
in South Street. Among the
artefacts to be removed to the
new town hall was a heraldic
panel dated 1565 and the town
bell, recast in 1697. This is now
rung to mark meetings of the
community council and the
death of eminent St Andreans.
The photograph was taken in
November 1969.

James S. Paton & Son, jewellers and opticians, is remembered for its good service and the ticking, chiming and striking of clocks (see page 27 for a close-up of the shop-front). The business subsequently moved from this location at 2 St Mary's Place to the west side of Bell Street. Duncan's Garage dated from the early days of motoring, and one of the services it provided was the recharging of the clumsy accumulators once used for wireless sets. In addition to their garage in St Mary's Place, Duncan's also had premises at 52 Argyle Street and one of the earliest telephones in St Andrews, No. 56. Other twentieth century St Andrews garages which are no longer trading (their former sites now occupied by housing) are Anderson's of Argyle Street, Hamilton's of the West Port, Johnston's of North Street, Culross's of Market Street, and Wilson's

of South Street and Alexandra Place. This photograph was taken in 1955, and today the early nineteenth century house from which Duncan's and Paton's traded – restored and renovated – is the university's chaplaincy centre. It has reverted to its original name of Mansefield and stands opposite the former West Infant School of 1844 (extended 1894), now local government offices. The Victoria Cafe, next door to Mansefield, was an elegant family restaurant with a tea-garden, waitress service and a large upstairs function room. The latter was accessed from the pillared doorway on the left. St Mary's Place takes its name from St Mary's Church, built in 1839 to supplement the seating in Holy Trinity Church. It still stands but is no longer a church. The street was part of the nineteenth expansion of St Andrews beyond its old burgh boundaries.

George Cowie took this photograph of the eighteenth century West Port House just before it was demolished in 1969. For many years it was the home of the Hamilton family, owners of the West Port Garage. The business was founded by Robert Hamilton, blacksmith (1869–1933). At one time his premises extended from the top of Melbourne Brae to the West Port and included a smithy, cycle shop, garage and petrol station. In the 1920s, when few people owned cars, the firm operated two open-top charabancs which were replaced by touring coaches in the 1930s. Walter Hamilton (Robert's son) collected a brand new super-deluxe 26-seater Bedford from Luton in 1935, driving it to St Andrews at the running-in speed of 30 mph. In 1938 the Hamilton coaches were sold to Alexander's and repainted in the Bluebird livery. Following Walter Hamilton's retiral in the late 1940s, the business was taken over by Alex Gillespie, the garage's head mechanic. Later it became solely a petrol station, and the house was demolished to increase the size of the forecourt. New housing now stands on the site. In addition to repairing agricultural machinery and shoeing horses, the Hamilton smithy designed and made ornamental lamps and stair railings for some of the larger houses in the town's western suburbs, as well as fencing for local council houses. Ironwork was also made for Mrs Younger of Mount Melville.

The windows of James S. Paton & Son dressed for the Coronation of Queen Elizabeth on 2 June 1953.

Queen Elizabeth was crowned on 2 June 1953 and St Andrews was en fête for the occasion, colourful with flags, bunting and beautifully dressed shop windows. Coronation parties were held everywhere, and a succession of special events took place. A united church service was held in Holy Trinity Church, and the latter's bells pealed at intervals throughout the day until nine o'clock in the evening. In those early days of television, some St Andrews households watched the Coronation on their black and white television sets. The day, which had been cold and grey, ended with a huge bonfire on the West Sands lit at 11 p.m. by Provost Jessie Moir, the first and only lady provost of St Andrews. She was elected to the town council in 1942 and became provost in 1952. Special Coronation copies of the New Testament, suitably inscribed, were gifted to schoolchildren by Fife County Council, while the town council gave local pupils special cakes of chocolate in decorated containers. George Cowie photographed this 1953 Coronation Day street party in Sandyhill Crescent. Notice the wedge shoes being worn by one mother. Today wedges are fashionable again.

The proclamation to mark the accession of Queen Elizabeth II to the throne was read in time-honoured fashion by town clerk Mr N. Mackenzie at St Andrews Market Cross. The ceremony took place at 2.30 on Saturday 9 February, and was attended by the town council in their civic robes, headed by Provost W. P. A. Tulloch. Also present was the university senate, led by the principal and vice-chancellor of St Andrews University Sir James Irvine. The senate had walked to the Cross in academic robes, preceded by the bearers of the university maces. Students followed in scarlet gowns. A year before the Jacobite rebellion of 1715, and in the same place and fashion, George I, the first of Britain's Hanoverian kings, was proclaimed king by the town clerk and by 'touck of drum' in the presence of the 'magistratts and councill' of St Andrews. There have been changes in this part of Market Street since the photograph was taken. The Cross Keys Hotel is a now a residential block, while the premises of the Royal Bank of Scotland (now in South Street) and the former British Linen Bank have been converted for other commercial purposes. Note the spectators in the background who have climbed on the fountain, a memorial to the novelist George Whyte Melville (1821–78). A prolific and successful writer, Melville was killed while hunting in Gloucestershire in 1878. He was the only son of John Whyte Melville and his wife Catherine, whose family home was Mount Melville. A well-known member of the Royal & Ancient Golf Club, John Whyte Melville was prominent in Fife affairs. The fountain provided drinking water for horses and dogs well within living memory.

This car mounted the pavement and ran into the window of J. & T. Rodger in South Street on a mid-August Sunday in 1961. Rodger's shop, now called the Meal Shop, occupied the former premises of A. Haxton & Co. (a well-remembered St Andrews grocer) from 1958. Cowie & Govan have now gone, as has R. Eddie, joiner, and the row of public phone boxes which were replaced by a shop. The telephone kiosks stand in front of the remaining (west) part of a large old house traditionally associated with Kate Dalrymple of the lively old Scots song of the same name. Kate's house has also seen some changes since 1961. From 1907 the main St Andrews post office occupied part of the Victorian building which stands on the site of the east part of Kate Dalrymple's house. Between 1848 and 1865 this was occupied by Dr John Adamson, co-founder of the town's first cottage hospital (opened in 1866 at 33 Abbey Street) and a skilled photographic pioneer. St Andreans traditionally brought in the new year in front of the post office, but the custom had all but died out by 1973. In 2008 the post office moved from this site to within W H Smith's.

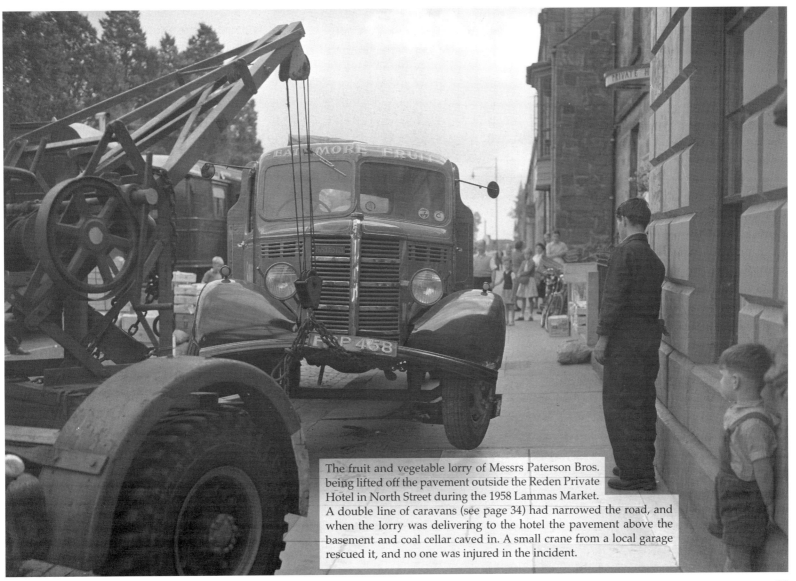

The fruit and vegetable lorry of Messrs Paterson Bros. being lifted off the pavement outside the Reden Private Hotel in North Street during the 1958 Lammas Market.

A double line of caravans (see page 34) had narrowed the road, and when the lorry was delivering to the hotel the pavement above the basement and coal cellar caved in. A small crane from a local garage rescued it, and no one was injured in the incident.

The Lammas Market underway in South Street in 1960. The old-fashioned roundabout in front of St Mary's College (founded 1537–54) featured hobby horses splendidly painted in the old fairground tradition with flaring red nostrils and barley sugar twisted poles to hang on to. The first of South Street's lime trees were planted on its north side by local property owners in 1879, and planting on the south side followed in 1880. The planting was suggested by John Milne (1823–1904), architect and councillor, who pioneered tree-planting in the streets of St Andrews to enhance the town.

Another Lammas Market photograph taken in South Street in 1960. Do you remember Mr di Folco's shop at 104 South Street (visible to the left of the BP sign above Central Motors), with its attractive period frontage? A grocer and confectioner's, it later became the premises of W. K. Chapman, jeweller. Today the premises still has its old fashioned frontage. Central Motors are now sited in Largo Road, and their former site has been redeveloped as housing called Southgait Close (Southgait/gate being the name of South Street between the fifteenth and eighteenth centuries). Note the carved and painted Masonic Lodge markings on the building to the right. Masons in St Andrews appear to have held their early meetings in various buildings in the town, but by 1820 this South Street building was known as the Masons' Old Lodge. On the institution of the Grand Lodge of Scotland in 1736, St Andrews was entered as No. 27, but later became No. 25. The photograph of Smith & Govan, referred to on page 14, was taken from a vantage point above or adjacent to Mr di Folco's shop. On the left is the corner turret of the present town hall, built in 1858–60 to replace the townhouse/tolbooth in Market Street. The turret contains the old town bell, which was recast in 1697.

Lammas Market caravans parked in North Street – a scene you wouldn't see in today's St Andrews! When passing the caravans, intriguing glimpses were caught through open doors of neat interiors with burnished stoves and colourful ornaments. Usually the finest of the caravans were those of the fortune-tellers. Often painted white or cream, their interiors gleamed and glittered with mirrors, crystal and chrome. Water for the caravans was carried and stored in big, shiny metal jugs and supplied by householders in North Street. Many of the same show-people came to the market year after year. On the right is a yet unfinished new College Gate, while prominent in the background is the tower of St Salvator's College. Its spire was added c.1550. The college, which is part of St Andrews University, was founded by Bishop James Kennedy in 1450.

A Lammas Market one-man-band captivates his audience in Market Street in 1970. Senior's shoe shop, in the background, subsequently moved to South Street and closed in January 2007. Also no longer trading in Market Street are Hill's Cleaning Centre and Joe Palompo's long-established and well-remembered cafe (beyond Senior's with the bow-windowed house above).

Above: A September 1961 photograph showing storm damage at Kinkell caravan site. This area was bought by the town council in 1939, but wasn't developed as a camping and caravan site until after the Second World War. It was officially named Kinkell caravan site in 1957, and that July, during the Glasgow Fair, about 2,000 holidaymakers were staying there in over 400 caravans. With an elevated location on the Kinkell Braes overlooking the East Sands, and fine views of the bay, harbour and town, it remains popular with holidaymakers today.

Right: Flood water in Lamond Drive, March 1976. The equivalent of four weeks rainfall (3.25 inches) fell in St Andrews over the second last weekend of March that year. A build-up of water swept through gardens and flooded roads in the town. It was considered to be the first real flood St Andrews had experienced for thirty years.

North Street, showing the properties at Nos. 19–21 in the process of being renovated. An interesting heraldic panel was found during the refurbishment of this old, pantiled building in the Ladyhead area. The renovation, which was completed in 1949, preserved the only example of a pillared forestair left in St Andrews. The tower and spire of St Salvator's College dominates the background of the photograph, which shows about three-quarters of the former Ladyhead fishing quarter. In the nineteenth century the Ladyhead was home to about 200 fisher families. Lines of haddock were hung up to dry, fishing nets were mended, mussels were shelled and lines baited outside these homes. The wall on the left marks the garden of Dean's Court, the old archdeacon's manse, reconstructed c.1570 by Sir George Douglas, who helped Mary, Queen of Scots, to escape from Loch Leven Castle. Northgait – later North Street – was one of the two impressive processional ways which converged on St Andrews Cathedral. The other was Southgait, later South Street.

This photograph and the one opposite were taken on 29 July 1950 and show the then annual motor race on the West Sands. The Lothian Car Club sponsored the thirty-mile event, and the 1950 winner (who was from Duns) was presented with his trophy by the film star Jean Kent. His average speed had been 60 mph.

The motor racing which once took place on the West Sands was closely connected with the former St Andrews & District Motor Club. Active club members included Alex Gillespie, who took over the West Port Garage from the Hamilton family (see page 26) and his brother Peter, a well-known local driving instructor. The club seems to have ceased meeting in the 1960s.

James (Jim) MacArthur baking shortbread in a high-pressure steam tube oven using a traditional long-handled baker's peel. The photograph was taken in 1958 at the premises of John W. MacArthur Ltd., 'bakers and confectioners of quality', 34 South Street. MacArthur's made St Andrews Scotch Shortbread, Kate Kennedy Shortbread Fingers, St Leonard's Shortbread Fingers, Royal and Ancient Shortbread and St Andrews 'Old Course' Shortbread. Packed in colourful tins and boxes, it was posted all over the world. Not for nothing was MacArthur's called the Shortbread House! The company was established by John W. MacArthur in 1892 and its shop and attached bakehouse stood at the junction of Abbey Street and South Street. The bakehouse was modernised in 1939 when 'spray baths' were installed for the bakers. Today 34 South Street is still a retail unit, although not a baker's shop, while the former bakehouse has been redeveloped as housing. The research of the late Dr R.G. Cant of St Andrews University revealed that the site of 34 South Street had been a bakery from the fifteenth century. MacArthur's also had a cafe and bakery at 116 South Street (see inside front cover).

Miss Winifred Wilson, aged 77, photographed in December 1960 distributing Christmas presents to children in South Street. Her father, George Wilson, inspector of the poor for St Andrews, had done the same in much earlier years. Known generally as 'Nurse Wilson', Winifred's nursing career took her to many parts of the world. She served in the First and Second World Wars and the Spanish Civil War. For a time she nursed in the Ballater area when the young Dukes of York (later Edward VIII) and Kent were among her patients. At one time matron of a leper colony in Cyprus, she was latterly with the Church of England's Melanesian Mission. During her years of retirement in St Andrews, Miss Wilson worked tirelessly for charity. To the right is the former Greenock Hosiery shop, which sold wools and knitted garments. Located at 137 South Street, it opened in 1939 as the Scotch Wool and Hosiery Stores of Fleming Reid & Co. Anderson's china and gift shop is behind the boys in Madras College uniforms. Just beyond Anderson's is the entrance to the Burgher Close, which contains the pantiled three-storey eighteenth century building used as a Burgher meeting house from 1774–86. This was restored by the St Andrews Preservation Trust in 1963.

Abbey Street is one of the oldest settled parts of St Andrews, and in the fifteenth century was known as Prior's Wynd. This photograph shows an archaeological dig in progress following the demolition of buildings on the north-east corner of Abbey Street and South Street. This took place during the 1969–70 widening of Abbey Street and the remains of a medieval timber house were found. The late-sixteenth or early-seventeenth century townhouse on the right was also discovered at the time. It had been hidden behind a much later South Street frontage. The house was renovated by St Andrews Preservation Trust with the support of the town council, but the close of small stone houses tucked away behind it didn't survive the widening of Abbey Street. St Andrews Co-operative Society's self-service grocery (in the background) was one of the first in the town. It incorporated a small butchery (not self-service) and traded into the 1970s. Until c.1850 the old Black Bull Inn stood on its site at 27 South Street. Once the principal stagecoach inn in St Andrews, it was the scene of regular golfing dinners and suppers. In 1884 it was described by George Bruce, author of the *Wrecks and Reminiscences of St Andrews Bay* as "that ever open haven of shipwrecked crews". After their rescue at the East Sands by St Andrews divinity student John Honey on 5 January 1800, the crew of the *Janet* of Macduff were taken to the Black Bull. In addition to its grocery, the St Andrews Co–op had two other premises in South Street selling ladies' fashions, babywear and children's clothes, household linens, furniture and electrical goods.

This George Cowie photograph, taken in January 1964, shows the old Shorehead buildings in the process of being rebuilt. There is an empty space where the Royal George tenement of cramped two-room (but and ben) fisher homes once stood. A nineteenth century conversion of a former granary, the Royal George was condemned and emptied of its occupants in 1935, but was not demolished until the 1960s when the Shorehead buildings were rebuilt as houses and flats. In this 1964 photograph only the former whitewashed Bell Rock Tavern (seen on the right of the photograph) is occupied. It was used as a house and studio by the well-known artists Josef and Roberta Sekalski. At the south end of the Shorehead buildings was the three-storey Auld Hoose pub (roofless on the left here). Adjoining it were the former coastguard office and store, and Mr Bonella's meal mill. The overcrowded Royal George was nicknamed after the 100 gun naval vessel of the same name which capsized on 29 August 1782 when lying at Spithead undergoing a repair. Almost all her crew were aboard, along with many visiting women and children. The crowded vessel sank almost immediately with great loss of life. Behind the space left by the Royal George is the two-storey building which belonged to the St Andrews Gas Co., now a house. From 1835 until February 1962, gas was made at the nearby St Andrews Gasworks. Higher up at East Kirkhill the old signal station can be seen. Much older than the bridge in the photograph, which links the Shorehead and the East Bents, were the stepping stones behind Balfour Place. They had the unusual name of Potty or Patty Lane, and could only be crossed when the harbour water was low.

This photograph of St Andrews United players and the one opposite are thought to date from the 1959–60 season. The players are Hugh Hay, George Davidson, Alan Ross (trainer), Jackie Smith, John Lister, William P. Penman, Thomas Carmichael, Charles Finlay, John Fraser, Thomas Wills, William Penman, Romeo Borella and John Keddie. The photos were taken at St Andrews FC's ground, Recreation Park in Langlands Road. The club was first mentioned during the season 1919–20 when they were one of the seven teams that played in the East Fife Junior League. They enjoyed very successful seasons in 1926–7, 1927–8 and 1928–9 when they won the Fife Junior League Championship three years running, the first team to do so.

In 1927–8 St Andrews FC were also the first winners of the Fife Cup, retaining the trophy the following year. A much-celebrated St Andrews football occasion took place in 1959–60 when the club won the Scottish Junior Cup at Hampden Park. They beat the favourites, Greenock Juniors, 3–1, and at that time were only the second Fife team to have won the Scottish Junior Cup since its inception in 1886. Jubilant crowds welcomed the victorious St Andrews United team on their return to the town with the cup, and the same evening they received a civic reception in the town hall. The goal-scorers were Romeo Borella (2) and William Penman. It is worth noting that this team had never played together before, nor did they ever do so again. To complete the 1959–60 season St Andrews also won the Fife League, Fife Cup and Rosslyn Cup. This picture shows, working back from the front, John Keddie, John Hughes, Thomas Wills, William Penman and Hugh Hay.

Alec Bayne of Macgregor's, Market Street, and Rachel Nicoll of Fletcher's, South Street, were voted 'sales assistants of the year' by St Andrews residents in 1975. The competition was inaugurated by the St Andrews Merchants' Association and was in its third year in 1975. Both of the shops where the winners worked originated in the nineteenth century and are well remembered by former customers. Macgregor's were house furnishers and had large furniture showrooms. They also sold carpets, other floor coverings and soft furnishings, employing their own carpet-layers and also running a removals business and auction rooms. In addition they were funeral directors. The two competition winners were presented with trophies at the annual dance of the St Andrews Merchants' Association.

Rachel Nicoll photographed in Fletcher's, 121 South Street, having won the 1975 sales assistant of the year competition. Fletcher's, which closed in 1983, had for many years sold all manner of toys, books, fancy goods, stationery and other printed matter. Dr Grierson's *Delineation of St Andrews*, which was printed by G.S. Tullis, carries the imprint 'Melville Fletcher, 1838'. No Christmas was complete for the youngest members of our family without a visit to a brightly lit Fletcher's after darkness had fallen to see the books and toys. The shop's little mechanical bird, which opened its beak and sang in its cage, was a particular highlight. Today the shop has been incorporated into other retail premises, but retains its fine period frontage with stained glass detailing and a mosaic step in cream, terracotta and blue.

Staff at the once-popular Royal Hotel pose behind a buffet in December 1954. Located at 118 South Street, the Royal was designed by local architect George Rae (1811–69) and completed in 1857. In the Victorian era it offered 'families, golfing, and commercial gentlemen' a 'high standard of comfort, good food, well-aired bedrooms, and private sitting rooms'. Having been acquired by the university in 1963, the Royal Hotel became Southgait Hall, a student residence. Additional student accommodation was built behind it in the area once used for coaching and garaging facilities. From 1983 Southgait Hall housed both St Leonard's College and the university staff club. In 1999 the university sold the building, and it has since been developed as private housing called Southgait Hall and Court. The house at 59–61 South Street still bears the name-plate of 'George Rae Architect'. Mr Rae also designed the Cross Keys Hotel in Market Street c.1850 (page 29) and its 1865 addition.

Construction of the university library in North Street in its very early stages. The new library, which opened in 1976, was built in the former grounds of St Katherine's School on a site bounded by The Scores to the north, Butts Wynd to the east, and North Street to the south. The architects were Williamson, Faulkner, Brown & Partners. On the left is the bulk of the New Picture House, opened in December 1930. It is one of Scotland's oldest independent cinemas and north-east Fife's last surviving picture house. Until 1838, when it was demolished, the city's Northgait Port stood just west of the cinema site. The New Picture House was built on the site of an old vernacular building with crow-stepped gables. Latterly used as a public hall, this stood with its gable end to the street and was once the home of a General Christie. The West Sands (featured in the 1981 film *Chariots of Fire*) and part of the Links can be seen in the distance.